YOSEMITE TRAVEL GUIDE 2024

The Comprehensive Travel Companion to Discover the Iconic Landscapes, Thrilling Hikes, Unforgettable Moments and Natural wonderland of Yosemite in 2024

BERNARD B. LENZ

Copyright © by Bernard B. Lenz

2024

All right reserved.

Thankful to you for consenting to protected innovation guidelines by downloading this book through genuine methods and by not replicating, checking, or spreading any piece of this book.

ABOUT THIS GUIDE

Embark on an extraordinary journey through the heart of **Yosemite with our 2024 Travel Guide**, a comprehensive companion designed to elevate your exploration of this natural wonderland. As you thumb through the pages, prepare to be captivated by the iconic landscapes that have drawn adventurers for generations.

This guide meticulously unveils Yosemite's breathtaking vistas, from the towering granite cliffs of El Capitan to the mesmerizing waterfalls of Bridalveil Fall. Immerse yourself in the enchanting beauty of Half Dome and witness the ever-changing colors of Yosemite Valley as the sun casts its magical glow upon the valley floor.

For the avid hiker, our guide presents a treasure trove of thrilling trails, each promising an exhilarating journey through diverse terrain. Whether you're a seasoned trekker seeking the challenge of the Mist Trail or a casual stroller exploring the serene meadows of Tuolumne Meadows, Yosemite offers a spectrum of hiking experiences for all skill levels.

Capture unforgettable moments as you traverse the park's diverse ecosystems, encountering wildlife like black bears, mule deer, and the elusive bobcat. Practical tips on photography and wildlife observation ensure that every nature enthusiast can make the most of their Yosemite adventure.

With insights on seasonal highlights, accommodation options, and dining recommendations, this guide ensures a seamless and enriching experience. Join us in 2024 as we explore Yosemite's natural wonders, where every turn unveils a new facet of this timeless landscape—a journey that promises to etch memories that will last a lifetime.

TABLE OF CONTENT

INTRODUCTION...........9
Welcome to Yosemite National Park..........9
Brief history and relevance.......................12

CHAPTER 1........................15
PLANNING YOUR TRIP......................15
The best time to visit............................15
Entry fees and permissions......................17
Accommodation choices........................... 20

CHAPTER 2........................23
GETTING THERE.......................... 23
Transportations Choices........................... 23
Driving instructions............................ 26
Public Transit.................................28

CHAPTER 3........................31
ACTIVITIES IN YOSEMITE.....................31

Hiking paths..31
Rock climbing... 34
Wildlife watching.. 36
Photography locations............................... 39

CHAPTER 4..**42**
ICONIC LANDMARKS............................. **42**
Yosemite Valley... 42
El Capitan... 45
Half Dome... 48
Glacier Point.. 50

CHAPTER 5..**54**
CAMPING IN YOSEMITE......................... **54**
Campground options................................. 54
Backcountry camping................................ 57
Reservation tips.. 59

CHAPTER 6.. **62**
DINING AND FOOD................................... **62**

Restaurants and cafés...................................... 62
Picnic places... 65
Food storage tips..67

CHAPTER 7..**70**
SAFETY AND REGULATIONS................... **70**
Park rules and regulations.......................... 70
Safety guidelines... 73
Emergency contacts..................................... 76

CHAPTER 8..**79**
WILDLIFE AND NATURE..........................**79**
Flora and wildlife guide............................... 79
Birdwatching locations................................82
Leave No Trace principles.......................... 84

CHAPTER 9..**87**
NEARBY ATTRACTIONS.......................... **87**
Mariposa Grove of Giant Sequoias............ 87
Mono Lake..90

Tuolumne Meadows..92

CHAPTER 10...**95**
EVENTS AND FESTIVALS.........................**95**
Annual events in Yosemite.........................95
Ranger-led programs...................................98

CHAPTER 11..**101**
SUSTAINABLE TOURISM......................**101**
Eco-friendly methods................................101
Responsible tourism advice....................104

CHAPTER 12..**107**
RESOURCES..**107**
Maps and guides..107
Useful websites..110
Visitor centers..112

CONCLUSION.. **115**

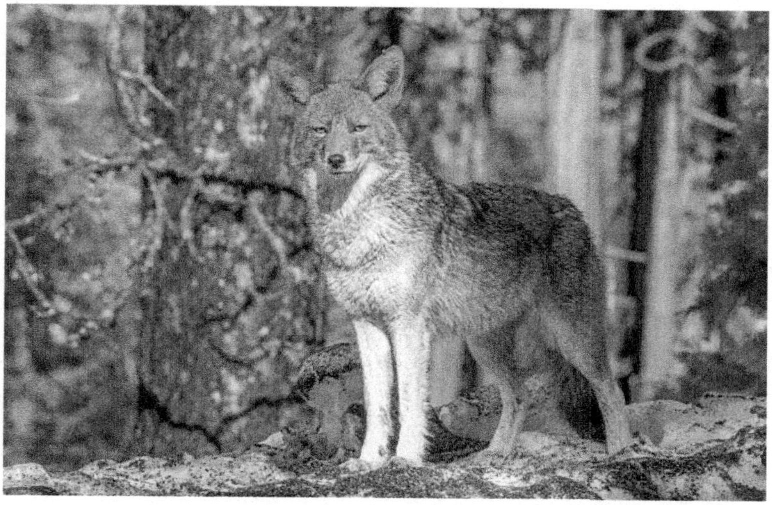

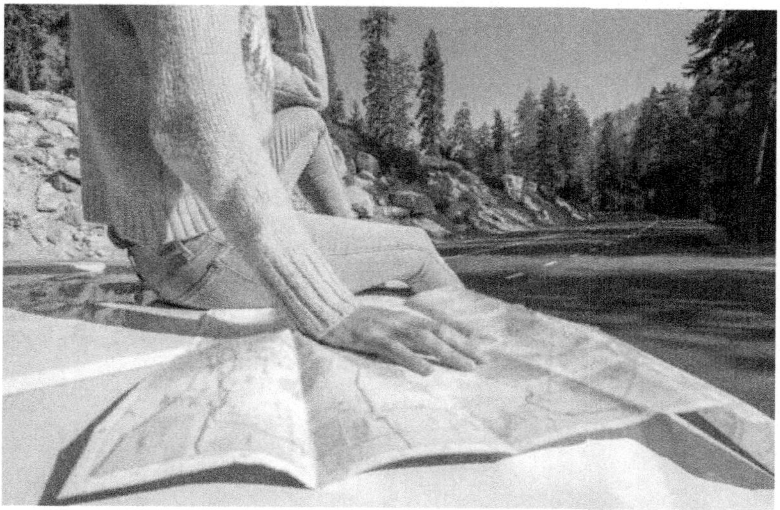

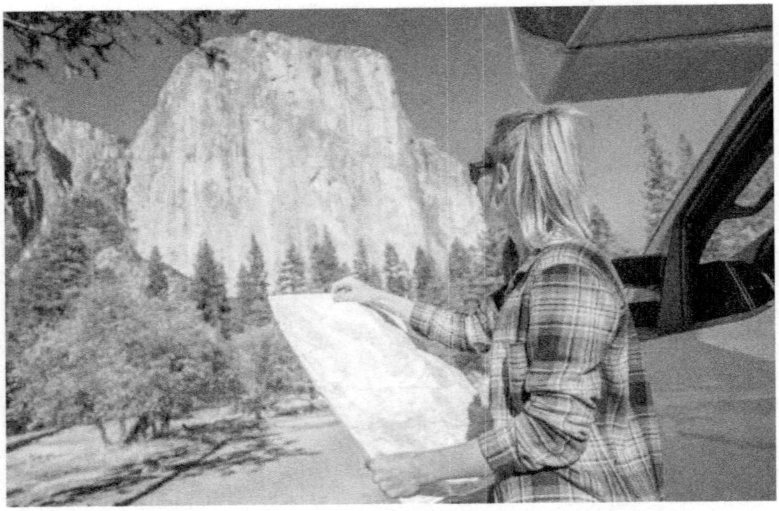

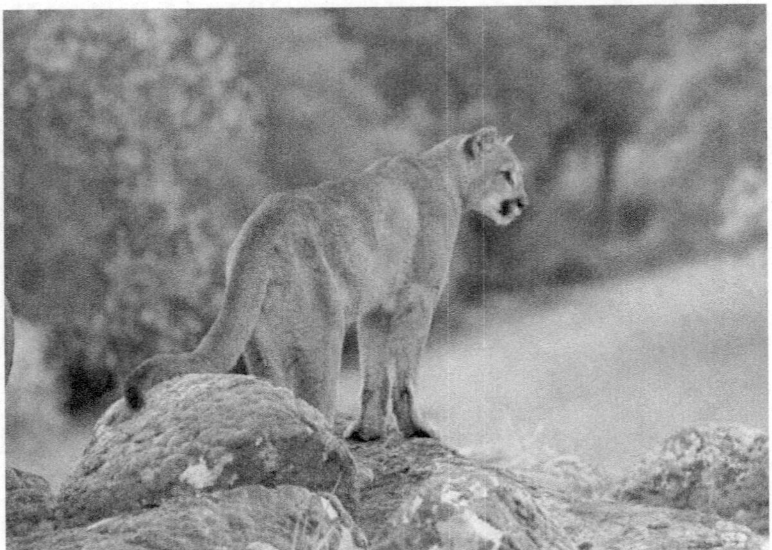

INTRODUCTION

Welcome to Yosemite National Park

It is a monument to the unadulterated beauty and amazing variety of nature that Yosemite National Park stands as a testament to. This historic park, which is located in the Sierra Nevada and encompasses more than 1,100 square miles, is a haven for outdoor enthusiasts who are looking for breathtaking scenery and unspoiled wilderness. Not only was it established in 1890, but it also bears the distinction of being one of the oldest national parks in the United States.

Yosemite Valley, a glacially sculpted sight that features towering cliffs, gushing waterfalls, and lush meadows, is the park's showpiece and is known all over the globe. It is the location of some of the most famous natural formations in the world, including El Capitan, a gigantic monolith made of granite, and Half Dome, a granite dome that has become a symbol of Yosemite National Park.

The various flora and wildlife of Yosemite National Park are a great example of the park's vast biological diversity. Located in Mariposa Grove, the park is home to some of the world's oldest enormous sequoia trees, which provide a peek into the history of the planet. Individuals who are interested in wildlife have the opportunity to see a wide range of creatures, such as black bears, mule deer, and a multitude of bird species.

Yosemite National Park is not just a natural wonderland, but it is also rich in cultural heritage. Because indigenous people, such as the Ahwahneechee, have considered this area their home for millennia, the park has several levels of cultural value.

As you commence on your adventure through Yosemite, expect to be fascinated by its majesty, calmness, and the intimate connection it creates with the natural world. Yosemite National Park is not only a destination; it's an immersing experience that leaves an unforgettable impact on those who explore its beauties.

Brief history and relevance

Yosemite National Park's history is as intriguing as its beauty. The park's story starts with indigenous peoples, particularly the Ahwahneechee, who lived together with the land for thousands of years. Their intimate connection to the region's natural splendor is interwoven in the park's cultural fabric.

In the mid-19th century, pioneers and adventurers, enticed by stories of Yosemite's beautiful grandeur, went into the region. Their descriptions, along with the mesmerizing photos of photographers like Ansel Adams, played a major part in the formation of Yosemite as a national park in 1890, conserving its magnificence for future generations.

The importance of Yosemite goes beyond its natural charm. It has been a beacon for conservation efforts, spurring the development of the National Park System. The notion of maintaining such pristine landscapes for human pleasure and ecological protection finds a champion in Yosemite.

Yosemite's granite cliffs, waterfalls, and various ecosystems contribute to its classification as a UNESCO World Heritage Site. The park serves not just as a paradise for outdoor lovers but also as a living laboratory for scientists researching ecology and geology.

Understanding Yosemite's history enriches the visitor's experience, developing awareness of the difficult balance between preservation and public access. As you explore its paths and marvel at its grandeur, realize that you are part of a tradition created by generations of admiration for the great beauty of Yosemite National Park.

CHAPTER 1

PLANNING YOUR TRIP

The best time to visit

Choosing the perfect time to visit Yosemite National Park is vital for optimizing your experience in its ever-changing seasons. Spring, from April to June, uncovers a rush of wildflowers and flowing waterfalls as the snow melts, while temperate temperatures make it a wonderful season for trekking and photography.

Summer, extending from July to September, is the peak season when the park teems with life. Warm temps allow up a choice of activities, from rock climbing to ranger-led programs. However, be prepared for crowds, and explore exploring lesser-known routes to avoid the rush.

Fall, from October to November, presents a stunning display of fall foliage, with fewer tourists compared to the warmer months. Crisp air and golden scenery create a calm setting for those preferring a gentler Yosemite experience.

Winter, from December to March, turns Yosemite into a snow-covered beauty. While certain places are shut due to snowfall, the winter months give chances for cross-country skiing and snowshoeing. The renowned Yosemite Valley, covered with a sprinkling of snow, takes on a calm appeal.

Ultimately, the greatest time to visit depends on your choices. If you love beautiful blossoms and pleasant temperatures, spring can be your best season. For a balance between activity and relaxation, autumn provides both. Consider the distinct offers of each season to customize your vacation to Yosemite's ever-changing natural rhythms.

Entry fees and permissions

Navigating the admission fees and permits for Yosemite National Park is necessary for a simple and legal visit. As of 2024, the park normally demands an admission fee, which funds conservation efforts and tourist services. The tariffs vary depending on the kind of vehicle or means of admission, with reduced pricing for seniors and yearly permits available for regular visitors.

In addition to entry costs, some activities inside the park may demand specific permissions. Backcountry camping, climbing, and some activities may need permits to minimize environmental damage and assure visitor safety. Planning and acquiring the appropriate permits improves your experience and contributes to the preservation of Yosemite's sensitive ecosystems.

Advanced reservation systems speed up the procedure for getting permits, especially for popular activities and lodgings. This guarantees that tourists can reserve their sites and enjoy Yosemite responsibly. It's essential to check the official park website or contact park officials for the most up-to-date information on fees, permits, and reservation systems, since rules may vary.

Understanding and complying with the admission fees and permission requirements not only assist a seamless entry into the park but also help the sustainable administration of Yosemite, conserving its natural beauties for decades to come.

Accommodation choices

Choosing the correct lodging is vital to optimizing your Yosemite experience, and the park provides several alternatives to suit various interests. Yosemite Valley has famous lodgings, offering easy access to the main sites. These historic lodgings provide a combination of luxury and accessibility to natural treasures.

For a more immersive experience, try camping at one of the campsites dotted around the park. Whether you prefer traditional tent camping or the comfort of RV sites, Yosemite's campsites enable you to interact with nature uniquely. Reservations are essential, particularly during high seasons.

For those seeking a balance between comfort and isolation, various cabins and holiday rentals are available both inside the park and in adjacent areas. These alternatives give a pleasant respite after a day of adventure.

For a backcountry excursion, Yosemite provides wilderness permits for overnight stays in the park's remote sections. This enables you to completely immerse yourself in the unspoiled nature, while adequate preparation and adherence to Leave No Trace rules are necessary.

Regardless of your hotel choice, reserving in advance is essential, particularly during high seasons. Whether you pick for the comfort of a lodge, the simplicity of camping, or the isolation of a cabin, choosing the correct lodging ensures that your time in Yosemite is as memorable as the beautiful vistas that surround you.

CHAPTER 2

GETTING THERE

Transportations Choices

Getting to Yosemite National Park is part of the trip, and numerous transportation alternatives cater to varied interests and demands. If you prefer the freedom of driving, entrance to Yosemite is feasible via well-maintained highways. The picturesque trip gives vistas of the surrounding landscapes, generating anticipation for the treasures inside the park.

For individuals who desire a more calm and eco-friendly approach, public transit choices are available. Buses and shuttles run from adjacent cities, giving a stress-free method to access the park. Once within Yosemite, a comprehensive shuttle system efficiently delivers tourists to important sites of interest, decreasing traffic and environmental impact.

If you're flying into the area, numerous airports serve as gates to Yosemite. From there, rental vehicles, shuttles, or private transportation services may continue the trip to the park.

For a unique and engaging experience, try visiting Yosemite by bicycle. The park offers bike routes, and riding gives a gentler pace, enabling you to absorb the beauty of the surroundings.

Understanding the transportation alternatives enables a seamless arrival and departure, enabling you to concentrate on the spectacular views and activities inside Yosemite. Whether you prefer the freedom of the open road, the ease of public transit, or the quiet of cycling, the route to Yosemite is as remarkable as the destination itself.

Driving instructions

Embarking on a road trip to Yosemite National Park uncovers a magnificent experience, and correct driving instructions are vital to navigating the enthralling route. If entering from the west, follow CA-140 for a lovely journey past Mariposa and into the famed Yosemite Valley. This approach uncovers stunning vistas and sets the setting for an awe-inspiring arrival.

Alternatively, from the south, tourists may use CA-41, bringing them past the historic village of Oakhurst before rising into the park. This route displays different landscapes and allows access to prominent attractions like Wawona and Glacier Point.

For visitors approaching from the east, CA-120 provides a magnificent journey across the high Sierra Nevada. As you pass across Tioga Pass, the tour unfolds with breathtaking sights, including the tranquil Tuolumne Meadows.

Navigating Yosemite's roadways needs cautious attention, especially in winter months when certain routes may shut due to snow. Checking road conditions and weather updates before your travel assures a pleasant drive.

These driving instructions not only lead tourists to the park's entrance but also give an introduction to the varied ecosystems and monuments around Yosemite. The drive becomes a vital part of the Yosemite experience, offering anticipation and amazement as you approach one of America's most renowned national parks.

Public Transit

For those wanting stress-free and eco-friendly travel to Yosemite National Park, public transportation alternatives offer a handy and sustainable alternative. Buses and shuttles run from many gateway areas, including Fresno and Merced, delivering a pleasant journey through gorgeous landscapes.

Yosemite's park-wide shuttle system significantly facilitates exploring inside the park itself. With various routes linking significant sites of interest, travelers can leave their automobiles behind and enjoy a seamless transportation experience. This not only decreases traffic congestion but also lessens the environmental effect, consistent with the park's dedication to sustainability.

During high seasons, the park's shuttle system becomes a vital resource, guaranteeing efficient and timely transportation. Whether you're traveling to Yosemite Valley, Glacier Point, or other renowned places, the shuttle system enables you to relax and immerse yourself in the natural splendor without the burden of parking.

For visitors traveling into the area, airports such as Fresno Yosemite International Airport and Merced Regional Airport serve as gateways to public transit choices. These mobility choices not only boost accessibility but also contribute to the preservation of Yosemite's beautiful environment, harmonizing with the idea of responsible tourism.

CHAPTER 3

ACTIVITIES IN YOSEMITE

Hiking paths

Yosemite National Park is a hiker's delight, featuring a variety of paths that run across varied environments, from towering sequoia trees to magnificent alpine meadows. The park's distinctive paths appeal to all kinds of hikers, giving possibilities for both simple strolls and strenuous climbs.

Beginners may find solace on the Yosemite Valley Loop Trail, giving panoramic views of renowned sights like El Capitan and Bridalveil Fall. For a more immersive experience, the Mist Trail, going to Vernal and Nevada Falls, captivates with misty cascades and beautiful surroundings.

Intermediate hikers may go onto the Glacier Point Trail, rewarding efforts with breathtaking panoramas of the High Sierra. Those wanting a day-long excursion could choose the Sentinel Dome Trail, concluding in a summit perspective that uncovers the park's magnificence.

Experienced hikers may attempt the Half Dome Trail, a hard climb culminating in stunning views from the peak. The John Muir Trail, covering over 200 miles, provides a more lengthy wilderness experience for seasoned trekkers.

Whether you're a newbie or a seasoned hiker, Yosemite's hiking routes give an intimate connection with nature. Be prepared with correct clothing, route maps, and an understanding of your selected path's difficulty to guarantee a safe and pleasurable tour through the amazing splendor of this historic national park.

Rock climbing

Yosemite National Park stands as a hotspot for rock climbers worldwide, with famous granite structures that challenge and inspire. The enormous cliffs, including the iconic El Capitan and Half Dome, lure climbers with their steep walls and complicated routes.

El Capitan, a vertical rock towering nearly 3,000 feet, is an ultimate test of skill and endurance. Climbers flock to its granite cliffs, with routes like "The Nose" and "The Dawn Wall" attaining legendary reputation in the climbing world. Scaling El Capitan is a peak feat in the world of rock climbing.

Half Dome, with its unusual rounded shape, provides the legendary "Snake Dike" route, delivering a unique combination of difficult climbing and exposure. The hike to the peak rewards climbers with magnificent views of Yosemite Valley.

For those new to climbing or wanting help, Yosemite provides a selection of climbing schools and guided trips. These programs cater to all ability levels, assuring a safe and pleasurable introduction to the art of climbing Yosemite's granite giants.

The park's dedication to maintaining its natural beauty is reflected in climbing rules, aimed to limit environmental effects. Climbers are advised to adopt Leave No Trace principles and obey seasonal restrictions to preserve breeding birds. Yosemite's rock climbing adventures epitomize the marriage of adventure and appreciation for the environment in one of the world's most legendary climbing sites.

Wildlife watching

Yosemite National Park's different ecosystems provide a shelter for wildlife, allowing visitors the opportunity to witness a rich tapestry of creatures in their native surroundings. From black bears to secretive bobcats, the park's woodlands and meadows teem with species, delivering a compelling experience for wildlife fans.

Yosemite Valley is an excellent site for observing charismatic megafauna such as mule deer and coyotes. Birdwatchers will enjoy an assortment of avian species, including the Peregrine Falcon and the Mountain Bluebird.

For a chance meeting with one of Yosemite's most famous inhabitants, the black bear, head into the park's quieter areas. Proper safeguards, including bear-aware habits and keeping food secure, allow a safe cohabitation with these majestic animals.

Tuolumne Meadows is another hotspot for animal watching, with possibilities to observe the secretive bobcat and the agile marmot. Patient watchers may even get a glimpse of the rare mountain lion, emphasizing the park's importance as a key home for these apex predators.

Guided wildlife tours and ranger-led programs give insights into the park's biodiversity, assuring a courteous and instructive wildlife-watching experience. Remember to remain at a safe distance and utilize binoculars or a telescopic lens for close observation, respecting the animals' natural habits. Yosemite's animal-watching possibilities allow interaction with the raw beauty of the park and appreciation of the fragile balance of its ecosystems.

Photography locations

Yosemite National Park is a photographer's dream, with an abundance of famous landscapes and natural marvels that have inspired artists for years. From dawn over Yosemite Valley to the alpenglow on Half Dome after sunset, the park provides an assortment of spectacular sights that demand to be recorded.

Yosemite Valley itself is a treasure mine of picture opportunity. Bridalveil Fall, with its ethereal mist capturing the early light, and El Capitan's granite monolith towering against the sky, produce classic compositions. Tunnel View, a renowned viewpoint, frames El Capitan, Half Dome, and Bridalveil Fall in a panoramic picture that embodies the majesty of Yosemite.

For intimate details and reflections, visit Mirror Lake, where the surrounding granite cliffs mirror the quiet waters, providing a tranquil and attractive backdrop. The quiet splendor of Sentinel Meadow, flanked by towering trees and the renowned Half

Dome in the background, provides a tranquil respite for contemplative photography.

Glacier Point, accessible by vehicle or foot, affords a spectacular vista of the High Sierra. Photographers throng here to capture the panoramic vistas, particularly after sunset when the warm colors shed a stunning light on the surrounding peaks.

Whether you're a skilled photographer or a casual fan, Yosemite's various vistas guarantee that every curve in the path presents a new and interesting composition. The park's ever-changing light and seasons provide a never-ending canvas for photographers looking to capture the soul of this natural marvel via their lens.

CHAPTER 4

ICONIC LANDMARKS

Yosemite Valley

Yosemite Valley serves as the pulsating heart of Yosemite National Park, a geological wonder created by glacial forces over millions of years. Surrounded by towering granite cliffs, this seven-mile-long canyon is a tribute to nature's beauty, mesmerizing everyone who enters with its spectacular sights.

El Capitan, an iconic monolith, demands attention as one of the world's biggest granite faces. Its intimidating appearance invites rock climbers from throughout the world to attempt to conquer its towering cliffs. Bridalveil Fall, with its gorgeous waterfalls, fills the valley, releasing a delicate mist that catches the sunlight, creating rainbows on bright days.

The iconic shape of Half Dome characterizes Yosemite's skyline. The granite dome, with its steep face and rounded contour, is a hard approach for hikers who brave the ropes to reach its peak, rewarded with spectacular panoramic views.

Tunnel View, a famous viewpoint, frames the valley's treasures in a single magnificent perspective. From this vantage point, tourists gaze at El Capitan, Bridalveil Fall, and the granite monoliths, appreciating the magnitude and majesty of Yosemite.

Sentinel Meadow, encircled by tall trees and watched over by Half Dome, provides a tranquil getaway. As seasons pass, the meadow alters, offering photographers and nature lovers with a canvas of hues and textures.

Yosemite Valley is not only a destination; it's an immersion into the amazing majesty of nature. Whether you're looking up at towering cliffs or exploring the valley floor, every aspect uncovers a new feature of this geological masterpiece, leaving an unforgettable impression on those lucky enough to see its marvels.

El Capitan

El Capitan, an iconic behemoth of Yosemite National Park, sits as a sentinel of granite, a symbol of power and beauty carved against the sky. Soaring almost 3,000 feet above the Yosemite Valley floor, this massive rock captivates tourists and climbers alike with its sheer vertical face.

Renowned in the climbing world, El Capitan's granite walls provide a tough challenge, drawing daredevils and pioneers since the mid-20th century.

Climbers from around the world come to test their talents on its steep face, with routes like "The Nose" and "The Dawn Wall" becoming renowned in the area of rock climbing.

As the sun sets, El Capitan undergoes a magnificent change, bathed in the warm tones of alpenglow. The granite sparkles with an ethereal light, creating a spell on visitors lucky enough to see this phenomenon.

Beyond its climbing attractiveness, El Capitan is a focus point for photographers who try to capture its magnificence against shifting backgrounds. From the green meadows in spring to the golden colors of fall, each season offers a particular appeal to this granite behemoth.

El Capitan isn't only a geological creation; it's a character in the tale of Yosemite, a mute witness to the passage of time. Whether you're an adventurous climber reaching its heights or an admirer staring up from the valley floor, El Capitan compels respect and adoration, leaving an unforgettable impact on those who experience its towering presence.

Half Dome

Rising magnificently from the Yosemite Valley, Half Dome is an iconic granite feature that serves as both a symbol of Yosemite National Park and a challenge for ardent hikers and climbers. This huge dome, with its unique half-dome form, dominates the park's skyline and is a monument to the awe-inspiring powers of nature.

For many, the fascination of Half Dome rests in the grueling but rewarding walk to its peak. The legendary Half Dome Trail, beginning at Yosemite Valley, goes through woodlands and granite expanses, ending at the iconic cable portion. Hikers scale steep granite cliffs, helped by the cables, to reach the peak where stunning panoramic vistas of the surrounding landscapes emerge.

The peculiar geology of Half Dome, formed by glacial and erosive processes, contributes to its mystery. The smooth granite surface and precipitous drop on one side generate a sensation of both vulnerability and victory for those who reach the peak. The granite behemoth is most attractive around sunset when the warm tones of alpenglow create a magnificent glow across its profile.

Photographers come to capture the various moods of Half Dome throughout the seasons, from the snowy crown in winter to the brilliant greens of spring and the golden colors of fall. Half Dome's importance goes beyond its physical appearance; it epitomizes the irrepressible spirit of exploration and adventure that distinguishes Yosemite National Park.

Glacier Point

Perched over 3,200 feet above Yosemite Valley, Glacier Point provides an unmatched vantage point, exposing visitors to a panoramic display of

Yosemite National Park's most renowned features. Accessible by automobile during the summer months and by cross-country skis or snowshoes in winter, this viewpoint affords a spectacular perspective of the park's majesty.

From Glacier Point, one may gaze at the towering granite monoliths, especially Half Dome, which stands as a beautiful sentinel against the background of the High Sierra. The cliffs of El Capitan and the flowing magnificence of Nevada and Vernal Falls are seen, presenting a full depiction of Yosemite's natural treasures.

Sunset at Glacier Point is a spectacular experience, with the warm colors of alpenglow showering the surrounding peaks. As the sun drops below the horizon, the landscape undergoes a dramatic metamorphosis, producing lengthy shadows and bathing the valley in a tranquil glow.

Beyond its breathtaking magnificence, Glacier Point plays a part in Yosemite's historic history. Early environmentalists, notably John Muir and Theodore Roosevelt, recognized its value in pushing for the preservation of the park. The Glacier Point Hotel, which previously existed at this beautiful overlook, attracted travelers seeking the awe-inspiring vistas.

Whether you come to Glacier Point in the warmth of summer or the stillness of winter, the experience is nothing short of awe-inspiring. It's a location where nature's majesty unfolds before your eyes, leaving an unforgettable impression of Yosemite's magnificence in your mind.

CHAPTER 5

CAMPING IN YOSEMITE

Campground options

Yosemite National Park provides several campsite alternatives, each giving a distinct experience among the park's magnificent surroundings. Yosemite Valley Campground, set amid renowned sites like El

Capitan and Bridalveil Fall, provides a central position with quick access to the valley's attractions. Reservations are generally suggested, particularly during busy seasons.

For a more quiet camping experience, Tuolumne Meadows Campground, located at a height of 8,600 feet, offers a tranquil respite surrounded by alpine meadows and granite peaks. This high-country campsite is suitable for those wanting a cooler environment and access to the park's less-explored sections.

Those wishing for a blend of convenience and environment might choose Wawona Campground, near the park's south gate. Surrounded by tall pine trees, it provides a serene environment and access to the Mariposa Grove of Giant Sequoias.

Backcountry camping aficionados may go on multi-day journeys, getting wilderness permits to camp in Yosemite's remote places. This provides for a more immersive experience, surrounded by the wild splendor of the park's different ecosystems.

Whether you like the comforts of conventional campsites or the serenity of backcountry camping, Yosemite has alternatives to fit every camping style. Planning, particularly for the popular campsites, assures a pleasant and comfortable stay in the middle of this natural splendor.

Backcountry camping

For those wanting a more immersive and adventurous experience, Yosemite National Park calls with its intriguing backcountry camping alternatives. Embracing the genuine spirit of discovery, backcountry camping enables guests to explore beyond the established routes and touch closely with the park's untamed environment.

Securing a wilderness permit is the key to accessing these hidden wonders. These licenses, attainable via a reservation system, control the amount of campers and help protect the sensitive ecosystems. From the challenging High Sierra routes to the calm meadows in the Yosemite Wilderness, backcountry aficionados may adapt their treks to varied landscapes and difficulty levels.

Backpackers are rewarded with isolation, unspoiled vistas, and the ability to experience the park's plants and creatures in their native settings. With careful preparation and respect to Leave No Trace principles, backcountry campers walk softly, ensuring minimum damage to the ecosystem.

As night sets, far away from artificial lights, the backcountry exposes a celestial spectacle, delivering a stunning astronomy experience. Whether you go on a multi-day trip or an overnight retreat, Yosemite's backcountry camping guarantees a true connection with nature, leaving travelers with unforgettable memories of the park's wild and untamed splendor.

Reservation tips

Securing reservations for camping in Yosemite is a critical step to ensuring a seamless and comfortable visit to this sought-after national park. Yosemite's popularity makes camping availability restricted, particularly during peak seasons, stressing the significance of smart preparation.

Plan Early: Yosemite campsites are in great demand, so it's wise to plan and reserve well in advance. Reservations for most campsites may be made up to six months ahead, and for others, demand is so strong that obtaining a place demands rapid action on the reservation system.

Be Flexible with Dates: If feasible, try altering your trip dates to maximize the probability of receiving a reservation. Mid-week stays frequently have greater availability compared to weekends.

Explore Lesser-Known Campgrounds: While Yosemite Valley Campground is popular, investigating lesser-known choices like Tuolumne Meadows or Wawona might enhance your chances of finding open campsites.

Utilize Shoulder Seasons: Visiting during the shoulder seasons, such as late spring or early autumn, provides good weather and improved availability, since the park tends to be less busy.

Monitor Cancellation Alerts: Stay cautious for last-minute cancellations. Yosemite's reservation system provides real-time availability updates, providing you the chance to secure a site if plans change for other campers.

By applying these reservation suggestions, you boost your chances of acquiring a place in one of Yosemite's campgrounds, assuring a wonderful and well-prepared camping experience in this beautiful natural marvel.

CHAPTER 6

DINING AND FOOD

Restaurants and cafés

Yosemite National Park provides a diversified gastronomic experience with a choice of restaurants and cafés that appeal to all tastes and preferences. Yosemite Valley provides various eating alternatives, including The Ahwahnee Eating Room, recognized for its exquisite environment and gourmet food that reflects the park's heritage. The Mountain Room Restaurant, located in the Yosemite Valley Lodge, serves full meals with spectacular views of Yosemite Falls.

For a more relaxed environment, the Yosemite Village Grill delivers a fast and enjoyable snack, excellent for fuelling up between expeditions. Degnan's Kitchen and Loft, near the tourist center, provides a range of selections, from deli sandwiches to wood-fired pizzas.

Tuolumne Meadows also provides food alternatives like the Tuolumne Meadows Grill, offering a handy stop for visitors hiking the high-country paths.

Additionally, Yosemite's eating facilities stress sustainability, with attempts to purchase locally and reduce environmental effects. It's important to check for seasonal menus and book reservations for popular eating venues, particularly during high visiting months. Whether enjoying a gourmet dinner with a vista or grabbing a quick snack on the run, Yosemite's restaurants and cafés contribute to a well-rounded and entertaining park experience.

Picnic places

Yosemite National Park allows tourists to explore the natural splendor while having a great picnic experience at its several designated picnic spots.

Scattered across the park, these sites offer perfect settings for a leisurely alfresco supper among towering trees, meadows, and renowned monuments.

Yosemite Valley, with its spectacular background of granite cliffs and waterfalls, provides various attractive picnic sites. Sentinel Beach Picnic Area near the Merced River and Cook's Meadow gives solitude and picturesque vistas, providing a pleasant ambiance for al fresco dining.

Wawona Meadow Picnic Area, near the historic Wawona Hotel, provides a serene respite with broad meadows and the distant background of the Sierra Nevada. In the upper altitudes, Tuolumne Meadows Picnic Area offers a quiet setting with the Tuolumne River trickling nearby, surrounded by the beauty of the High Sierra.

Visitors may bring their picnic or select refreshments from the park's eating outlets. These picnic sites, furnished with tables and occasionally grills, are great for families, hikers, and anybody wanting a rest surrounded by Yosemite's natural treasures. It's advised to come early, particularly during peak seasons, to get a great picnic place and savor a lovely dinner among the park's unrivaled splendor.

Food storage tips

When touring Yosemite National Park, reasonable food storage methods are vital to guarantee the safety of both tourists and animals. Yosemite's various ecosystems are home to black bears and other species, and incorrect food storage may draw them to human areas, putting both animals and humans in danger. Follow these food storage techniques for a safe and happy experience:

Use Bear-Resistant Food Containers: Yosemite requires guests to keep all food, toiletries, and scented goods in bear-resistant food canisters. These canisters are intended to resist a bear's efforts to get the contents, safeguarding both animals and park visitors.

Put products Properly in Vehicles: If you are staying in a car-accessible location, put food and scented products out of sight in a secured vehicle. Bears are skilled at breaking into automobiles if they smell appealing odors.

Be Mindful of Scents: Avoid bringing highly scented goods into the park. This includes fragrances, lotions, and even scented products. Bears have a good sense of smell and may be drawn from a significant distance.

Dispose of Trash Properly: Use authorized bear-resistant trash bins or dumpsters for disposing of rubbish. Never leave garbage or food leftovers at your campsite or along the pathways.

By following these food storage rules, visitors assist in the protection of Yosemite's animals and guarantee a safer and more pleasurable experience for those who explore this beautiful natural habitat.

CHAPTER 7

SAFETY AND REGULATIONS

Park rules and regulations

Yosemite National Park, known for its natural beauty, survives on the devotion of tourists to conserve its ecosystems and traditions. Understanding and following park laws and regulations is vital for a safe, happy, and sustainable experience:

Leave No Trace: Follow Leave No Trace principles to limit your influence on the environment. Pack out all litter, remain on authorized pathways, and respect animal habitats.

Wildlife Viewing: Keep a safe distance from wildlife, particularly bigger species like bears. Never feed animals, since it disturbs their natural behavior and endangers both them and you.

Campfire restrictions: Abide by campfire restrictions, which vary depending on location and time of year. In particular seasons, burning is restricted to avoid wildfires, and the use of portable stoves is suggested.

Speed restrictions: Adhere to stated speed restrictions throughout the park to protect the safety of both animals and tourists. Watch for animals crossing roadways, particularly at dawn and dusk.

Permit Requirements: Obtain essential permissions for activities like backcountry camping, rock climbing, and some events. This helps control environmental effects and guarantees safety.

Respect Cultural and Natural Resources: Show respect for the park's cultural and natural resources. Avoid touching or climbing on cultural elements, and do not destroy or remove any plants, rocks, or antiques.

By observing these laws and restrictions, visitors help the preservation of Yosemite National Park, ensuring its magnificence continues for years to come.

Safety guidelines

Ensuring a safe visit to Yosemite National Park entails being attentive to the various topography, animals, and constantly changing weather conditions. Follow these safety precautions for a secure and pleasurable experience:

Trail Etiquette: Stay on authorized paths to maintain ecosystems and limit the danger of getting lost. Inform someone about your intentions if you start on longer treks.

Weather Awareness: Yosemite's weather may change suddenly. Dress in layers, bring rain gear and be prepared for fluctuating temperatures, particularly at higher altitudes.

Animals Caution: Maintain a safe distance from animals, especially bears. Store food correctly to prevent drawing animals to campsites.

Water Safety: If indulging in water activities, be aware of rapid currents and chilly temperatures, particularly in rivers and lakes. Follow all safety requirements when swimming, and use life jackets as required.

Altitude Considerations: Yosemite's altitudes may reach above 13,000 feet. Take time to adjust, remain hydrated, and detect signs of altitude sickness.

Emergency Preparedness: Familiarize yourself with park emergency protocols, carry a basic first aid kit, and know the location of park emergency services.

Road Safety: Adhere to speed restrictions, check for animals on roadways, and be careful on curving mountain routes.

Prioritizing safety enriches the Yosemite experience, enabling visitors to fully enjoy the park's splendor while reducing hazards associated with its dynamic and often demanding environment.

Emergency contacts

Being informed of emergency contacts is vital for a safe and prepared visit to Yosemite National Park. In case of emergency, swiftly reaching out to the proper authorities may make a major difference. Key contacts include:

Emergency Services: For urgent help in any life-threatening crisis, phone 911. Provide specific information about your location and the nature of the situation.

Park Emergency Dispatch: Yosemite National Park has its emergency dispatch facility. Call 209-379-1992 for non-life-threatening events needing park rangers' intervention.

Visitor Centers: Yosemite's many visitor centers may give information and help. The Valley Visitor Center (209-372-0200) and Tuolumne Meadows Visitor Center (209-372-0260) are key resources.

Medical Facilities: Yosemite Medical Clinic, situated in Yosemite Valley, provides medical services. In case of a medical emergency, call the clinic at 209-372-4637.

Road Conditions: Stay updated about road conditions by contacting the 24-hour road and weather information line at 209-372-0200.

It's recommended to program these contacts into your phone and acquaint yourself with the locations of park services and medical facilities. Preparedness and prompt contact with authorized authorities help to a safer and more secure visit to Yosemite National Park.

CHAPTER 8

WILDLIFE AND NATURE

Flora and wildlife guide

Exploring Yosemite National Park gives a wonderful chance to experience varied flora and wildlife, adding to the park's biological diversity. Here's a quick introduction to some of the fascinating species you may encounter:

Flora: Yosemite exhibits a range of plant life, from towering sequoias to fragile wildflowers. The Giant Sequoias in Mariposa Grove and Tuolumne Grove are awe-inspiring giants, while meadows explode with color throughout spring and summer, presenting brilliant flowers like lupines and paintbrushes. Ponderosa pines, incense cedars, and Jeffrey pines dominate the wooded regions.

Fauna: Wildlife abounds in Yosemite, including famous species such as black bears, mule deer, and bobcats. Birdwatchers delight in observing peregrine falcons, Steller's jays, and the uncommon mountain bluebird. Yosemite is also home to several reptiles and amphibians, including the Western fence lizard and the Pacific tree frog.

Remember to see animals from a safe distance and stick to ethical viewing methods to prevent disturbance. Understanding the park's flora and wildlife helps the understanding of Yosemite's complicated ecosystems, offering a deeper connection to its natural grandeur.

Birdwatching locations

Yosemite National Park is a sanctuary for birding aficionados, featuring different habitats that attract a diversity of avian species. Here are some good birding areas inside the park:

Yosemite Valley: The meadows and forests of Yosemite Valley attract a variety of birds. Look for Steller's jays, American dippers near water, and the brilliant Western tanager during the warmer months.

Tuolumne Meadows: This high-country location gives a unique birding experience. Scan the sky for the magnificent golden eagle, then explore the meadows to discover mountain bluebirds, yellow warblers, and the secretive White-crowned sparrow.

Wawona: The various ecosystems surrounding Wawona, notably the Mariposa Grove, attract a diversity of bird species. Keep a watch out for the Pileated woodpecker, mountain chickadee, and the beautiful mountain bluebird.

Hetch Hetchy: The reservoir and surrounding landscapes at Hetch Hetchy attract waterfowl, making it a good site for seeing ducks, mergansers, and the odd osprey.

Bring binoculars and a field guide to improve your birding experience. As you visit these areas, you'll not only see a multitude of feathered inhabitants but also develop a greater understanding of the vast biodiversity that flourishes in Yosemite National Park.

Leave No Trace principles

Respecting and protecting the natural beauty of Yosemite National Park is vital for sustained enjoyment. The Leave No Trace principles encourage visitors to limit their environmental effect, guaranteeing the preservation of the park's natural wonders:

Plan Ahead and Prepare: Thorough preparation involves studying legislation, acquiring essential permissions, and being mindful of weather conditions to ensure a safe and responsible visit.

Travel and Camp on Durable Surfaces: Stick to established paths and campsites to minimize soil erosion and harm to delicate ecosystems. Avoid trampling on plants, particularly in meadows and high-use areas.

Dispose of Waste Properly: Carry away any garbage, leftover food, and litter. Utilize certified garbage disposal facilities and follow specified criteria for waste, including human waste in remote locations.

Leave What You Find: Preserve the park's natural and cultural treasures by avoiding damaging animals, vegetation, or historic buildings. Take just memories and images.

Minimize Campfire Impact: Follow restrictions governing campfires, utilize designated fire rings, and consider using a camping stove instead. Be aware of fire restrictions and their relevance in avoiding wildfires.

Respect animals: Observe animals from a safe distance, avoiding any acts that may affect their normal behavior. Do not feed animals, since it affects their diets and habits.

By following these Leave No Trace principles, visitors help the conservation and maintenance of Yosemite's ecosystems, ensuring future generations may marvel at the park's extraordinary splendor.

CHAPTER 9

NEARBY ATTRACTIONS

Mariposa Grove of Giant Sequoias

Nestled in the southern area of Yosemite National Park, the Mariposa Grove remains a stunning tribute to the eternal majesty of nature. Home to approximately 500 mature big sequoias, including the legendary Grizzly Big and California Tunnel Tree, this ancient forest captivates tourists with its awe-inspiring grandeur.

The Grizzly Giant, believed to be over 1,800 years old, demands attention as one of the oldest and biggest sequoias in the forest. Its huge limbs and towering presence generate a feeling of awe and amazement. The California Tunnel Tree, while no longer alive, offers a unique path through its gigantic trunk, affording an insight into the history of early preservation attempts.

Traversing the Mariposa Grove, tourists discover a network of routes weaving across this ancient woodland. The quietude is shattered only by the odd chirp of a bird or the whispering wind through the high trees. Interpretive programs and guided walks enhance the experience, bringing insights into the ecology, history, and protection of these unique trees.

Preservation efforts have developed throughout the years, stressing a careful balance between accessibility and conservation. Shuttle systems prevent human influence, enabling visitors to gaze at these living giants while guaranteeing the grove's future. The Mariposa Grove of Giant Sequoias draws everyone who comes to experience the lasting enchantment of these ancient sentinels, leaving an unforgettable impact on the hearts of anyone lucky enough to travel through this living cathedral of nature.

Mono Lake

Nestled against the magnificent background of the Eastern Sierra, Mono Lake stands as a unique and ancient gem amid California's varied geography. This salty lake, one of the oldest in North America, possesses great biological value and a dreamlike beauty.

What distinguishes Mono Lake is its extreme salinity and alkalinity, producing an environment where only specialized creatures can flourish. The lake provides an important home for millions of migrating birds, including California gulls and eared grebes, making it a vital stop along the Pacific Flyway.

The distinctive tufa towers, limestone structures that rise from the lake's surface, contribute to Mono Lake's unearthly charm. These towering formations are generated by the combination of freshwater springs and alkaline lake water, producing a stunning scene.

Efforts in the late 20th century to protect Mono Lake gained major attention. The Mono Lake Committee played a vital role in campaigning for water conservation and preservation, resulting in actions that helped restore the lake's water levels and secure the continuing health of its ecosystem.

Mono Lake, with its unique ecosystem and magnificent views, serves as a monument to the difficult balance between conservation and human activity in our natural marvels. Visitors to this high-altitude refuge observe a landscape that has persisted for generations, adding to the rich fabric of California's wildness.

Tuolumne Meadows

Tuolumne Meadows, located at a height of 8,600 feet in Yosemite National Park, opens as a beautiful alpine meadow surrounded by granite peaks, pure rivers, and brilliant wildflowers. This high-country retreat provides a dramatic contrast to the famed

Yosemite Valley, giving a tranquil respite for wildlife aficionados.

Bounded by the Cathedral Range to the east and the Sierra Nevada to the west, Tuolumne Meadows provides a gateway to a plethora of hiking paths, including routes to Gaylor Lakes, Lembert Dome, and the Pacific Crest Trail. The Tuolumne River meanders through the meadows, offering calm times along its banks.

The meadows explode into a blaze of hues throughout the brief summer season, presenting a varied assortment of wildflowers. Tuolumne's alpine habitat supports a multitude of species, from marmots and pikas to the rare black bear.

Campers wanting a quieter and cooler escape frequently select Tuolumne Meadows Campground. Nearby attractions like the Tuolumne Meadows Visitor Center and the historic Tioga Road, which weaves its way across the high country, add to the attractiveness of this alpine haven. Tuolumne

Meadows serves as a tribute to the enormous grandeur and variety that flourishes in the upper altitudes of Yosemite National Park, giving a calm retreat for those who seek a different element of the park's magnificence.

CHAPTER 10

EVENTS AND FESTIVALS

Annual events in Yosemite

Yosemite National Park conducts a range of yearly activities that bring visitors closer to nature, highlight the park's rich past, and build a feeling of community. Among these occurrences, the following stand out:

Yosemite Facelift: This environmental project urges volunteers to assist clean up and protecting the park each September. Participants participate in trail and roadside cleanups, encouraging stewardship and environmental responsibility.

Yosemite Valley Stargazing sessions: Held periodically, these sessions allow marveling at the night sky's beauty. Stargazers and astronomers join together to exchange knowledge and enthusiasm for the cosmic grandeur of Yosemite.

Earth Day Festival: Celebrated in April, Yosemite's Earth Day Festival stresses environmental education and sustainable behaviors. Workshops, events, and displays emphasize conservation initiatives and urge visitors to reduce their ecological imprint.

Ansel Adams Gallery Workshops: Throughout the year, photography lovers may participate in workshops provided by the Ansel Adams Gallery.

These activities give a chance to enhance photography abilities while photographing the park's magnificent vistas.

These yearly activities in Yosemite Z allow visitors to connect with the park's natural marvels, learn from experts, and contribute to its preservation. Whether cleaning up trails, stargazing beneath the great sky, commemorating Earth Day, or improving photography skills, these activities enrich the Yosemite experience, building a deeper connection to its unique and awe-inspiring attractions.

Ranger-led programs

Yosemite National Area's ranger-led programs provide visitors an opportunity to enhance their relationship with the area via expert-guided activities. These educational and interesting events appeal to a variety of interests and ages, increasing the overall Yosemite experience.

From informative tours to campfire lectures, rangers offer their substantial expertise about the park's geology, vegetation, animals, and cultural history. These programs generally take place in prominent sites such as Yosemite Valley, Tuolumne Meadows, and Mariposa Grove of Giant Sequoias.

For the most daring, guided treks explore lesser-known pathways, gaining insights into the park's various ecosystems. Stargazing events uncover the cosmic marvels above, taking advantage of Yosemite's beautiful night sky.

Children and families may engage in participatory Junior Ranger programs, developing environmental knowledge and a feeling of responsibility among the younger generation.

These ranger-led workshops not only boost comprehension but also foster a genuine respect for Yosemite's natural and cultural assets. The dedication and skill of Yosemite's rangers serve as a bridge between the park's marvels and its visitors, generating unique and instructive encounters that contribute to the continuing legacy of conservation and respect for this renowned national treasure.

CHAPTER 11

SUSTAINABLE TOURISM

Eco-friendly methods

Yosemite National Park promotes and advocates eco-friendly methods to maintain its sensitive ecosystems and limit the environmental effects of its millions of yearly tourists. These approaches coincide with the park's dedication to sustainability and conservation:

Waste Reduction: Visitors are asked to follow the "pack it in, pack it out" philosophy, bringing out all rubbish and limiting single-use goods. Recycling and composting facilities are accessible throughout the park.

Water Conservation: Yosemite encourages water conservation to safeguard its rivers and lakes. Visitors are advised to use water sensibly, report leaks, and stick to standards for water consumption.

Alternative Transportation: The park promotes the use of shuttle buses, bicycles, and electric cars to minimize air pollution and traffic congestion. Exploring Yosemite without personal automobiles decreases the carbon imprint.

Leave No Trace: Yosemite supports Leave No Trace principles, stressing responsible recreation, trail etiquette, and wildlife respect. These guidelines encourage visitors to enjoy the park while protecting its natural beauty.

Green construction Initiatives: Yosemite utilizes sustainable construction methods, including energy-efficient designs and the use of eco-friendly materials, in developing and maintaining structures.

By employing eco-friendly techniques, Yosemite attempts to maintain a harmonic balance between tourist delight and environmental preservation. Visitors are partners in preserving the park's longevity, contributing to the legacy of responsible care for years to come.

Responsible tourism advice

Responsible tourism is vital to preserve the natural beauty and ecological integrity of Yosemite National Park. Visitors may assist in conservation efforts and improve their own experiences by embracing the following responsible tourism tips:

Educate Yourself: Learn about the park's ecosystem, history, and Leave No Trace principles before coming. Understanding the unique ecosystem of Yosemite provides for a more meaningful and courteous experience.

Stay on Designated pathways: Stick to existing pathways to reduce soil erosion and safeguard sensitive ecosystems. Avoid shortcuts that may destroy plants and disturb animal habitats.

Respect animals: Maintain a safe distance from animals and never feed them. Observing animals from afar enables them to demonstrate natural behaviors and prevents habituation to human presence.

Reduce Waste: Carry a reusable water bottle, utilize eco-friendly goods, and pack away all rubbish. Minimize your environmental effects by leaving no evidence of your stay.

Conserve Water: Be aware of water consumption, particularly in camping and leisure activities. Follow park recommendations for water conservation and report any leaks.

Support Sustainable Practices: Choose eco-friendly hotels, utilize public transit or park shuttles, and choose sustainable items to support companies that promote environmental stewardship.

By implementing these responsible tourism practices, tourists play a critical part in protecting Yosemite's ecological balance and ensuring that this natural marvel remains a flourishing and treasured destination for years to come.

CHAPTER 12

RESOURCES

Maps and guides

Yosemite National Park, with its vast and varied landscapes, provides tourists with a selection of maps and guides to assist their exploration and comprehension of this renowned place. These resources play a crucial role in creating a smooth and enjoyable experience:

Park Maps: Yosemite offers comprehensive maps that emphasize significant sites of interest, trails, camps, and services. Available both online and at park gates, these maps serve as vital companions for traversing the park's enormous landscape.

Trail Guides: Comprehensive trail guides give insights into the park's numerous hiking opportunities. Ranging from casual strolls to hard backcountry treks, these guides include information on trail length, complexity, and prominent features.

Visitor Centers: Yosemite's visitor centers serve as hubs for information, giving maps, guides, and trained rangers eager to help. These facilities also hold exhibits and events that increase visitors' awareness of the park.

Digital applications: Technological improvements have given birth to digital maps and applications, offering real-time information about trails, areas of interest, and current conditions. These technologies provide ease for tech-savvy visitors seeking interactive and up-to-date content.

Whether it's a paper map, a trail guide, or a digital app, having the correct maps and guides ensures that visitors can traverse Yosemite's marvels with confidence, making the most of their time while immersing themselves in the park's natural majesty.

Useful websites

Navigating the marvels of Yosemite National Park is made more accessible by a range of educational and helpful websites. These online services provide tourists with vital information, travel planning tools, and real-time updates:

National Park Service (NPS) Website: The official NPS site for Yosemite contains complete information on park rules, permits, and current conditions. Visitors may obtain maps, and trail guides, and hear about ranger-led activities.

Yosemite Conservancy: Dedicated to sustaining the park, the Yosemite Conservancy's website gives insights into current conservation activities, educational programs, and possibilities for visitor interaction.

Recreation.gov: This portal supports campsite bookings, enabling a streamlined planning process for individuals wishing to reserve a space in Yosemite's famous campgrounds.

Yosemite Hospitality: Operated by Aramark, this site gives data on housing, food, and activities inside the park. It's a useful resource for individuals seeking hotel alternatives and investigating food possibilities.

Weather and Road Conditions: Stay current on weather predictions and road conditions via websites like the National Weather Service and the California

Department of Transportation. Timely information assists in planning and readiness.

Utilizing these resources offers Yosemite explorers the information required for a well-prepared and engaging stay, whether it's comprehending park restrictions or getting reservations for popular activities and lodgings.

Visitor centers

Yosemite National Park includes strategically positioned visitor centers that serve as informational portals to the park's stunning scenery and rich natural history. These centers play a key role in enriching the visiting experience:

Yosemite Valley Visitor facility: Situated in the middle of Yosemite Valley, this facility provides a multitude of services, including maps, exhibitions, and experienced rangers. Visitors may acquire crucial information, attend ranger lectures, and dig into displays displaying the park's geology and vegetation.

Tuolumne Meadows Visitor facility: Nestled in the high-country Tuolumne Meadows, this facility caters to people visiting the park's alpine zones. It gives insights into the distinct ecosystems of the region, trail information, and educational displays.

Wawona Visitor facility: Located near the Mariposa Grove of Giant Sequoias, this facility gives a warm welcome to tourists visiting the southern regions of the park. Informative exhibits illustrate the park's past, particularly its cultural heritage.

Hetch Hetchy Entrance Station: Serving people entering Yosemite from the Hetch Hetchy area, this station gives critical information on the park's less busy but still magnificent scenery.

These visitor centers serve as hubs of information, ensuring that guests begin their Yosemite experience well-prepared and educated. The committed rangers and displays help to a greater awareness of the park's natural beauty and cultural importance.

CONCLUSION

In concluding this Yosemite Travel Guide for 2024, we invite you to embark on an adventure that transcends the ordinary and taps into the extraordinary. Yosemite, with its iconic landscapes, thrilling hikes, and unforgettable moments, stands as a testament to the awe-inspiring beauty of the natural world.

As you traverse the pages of this comprehensive companion, envision the grandeur of Yosemite's granite peaks, the serenity of its meadows, and the power of its cascading waterfalls. Whether you're a seasoned explorer or a first-time visitor, let the guide be your compass, unveiling the wonders that make Yosemite a true natural wonderland.

In the heart of this majestic park, find not only an escape into the wilderness but a connection to the essence of nature itself. Capture the beauty through your lens, feel the exhilaration of conquering a challenging trail, and cherish the quiet moments when the magnificence of Yosemite speaks to your soul.

May this guide be your trusted companion, offering practical insights, tips, and inspiration for an immersive Yosemite experience. In 2024, let the landscapes of Yosemite be your canvas, and the adventures within its boundaries be your brushstrokes on the canvas of memories. The journey awaits, immerse yourself in the unparalleled magic of Yosemite and create a chapter in your travel story that will resonate with wonder for years to come.

We invite you to share your experiences and impressions by leaving a review and rating. Your feedback is invaluable in helping us continue to improve and inspire future travelers to explore Yosemite's unparalleled beauty. Thank you for choosing us, and happy exploring!

Printed in Great Britain
by Amazon